Susie Barber is an esteemed New Zealand-based author, known for her captivating works of historical non-fiction. Drawing inspiration from the life and legacy of Elizabeth I, Barber's writing delves into the intricacies of the past, illuminating forgotten stories and shedding light on defining moments in history.

With a keen eye for detail and a dedication to meticulous research, Barber's works transport readers to bygone eras, offering a fresh perspective on the events that have shaped our world. Her passion for historical accuracy is evident on every page, as she skilfully weaves together facts and narratives to create compelling and thought-provoking works.

When not immersed in the world of writing, Susie Barber can be found indulging in her love for reading, perusing the latest novels and historical texts. An avid collector of shoes, she also enjoys exploring the world of fashion and its impact on different periods. In addition, Barber is recognised as an expert in etiquette, a passion that adds depth and authenticity to her historical non-fiction works.

With a distinguished literary career spanning decade, Susie Barber continues to captivate audiences with her evocative storytelling and commitment to preserving the past through the written word. Her works stand as a testament to her unwavering dedication to historical scholarship and her enduring influence on the field of non-fiction literature. Insight makes her writing a must read to anyone with an interest in history, women's rights, and the stories of those who came before us.

Susie perfects the art of proper etiquette, brings a unique and humours perspective to her writing, and her quirky sense of humour shines through in every page. So, if you're in the mood for a good laugh and a history lesson all rolled into one grab one of Susie's books to be entertained.

For my loving husband, Paul Barber (Paulie); my confidante, my muse, my rock, my love.

Susie Barber

DEATH ROW

AUSTIN MACAULEY PUBLISHERS®
LONDON • CAMBRIDGE • NEW YORK • SHARJAH

A CIP catalogue record for this title is available from the British Library.

ISBN 9781035875665 (Paperback)
ISBN 9781035875672 (ePub e-book)

www.austinmacauley.com

First Published 2024
Austin Macauley Publishers Ltd®
1 Canada Square
Canary Wharf
London
E14 5AA

Table of Contents

Chapter 1
The Condemned

Life Before Death Row

The subchapter *Life Before Death Row* explores the lives of individuals prior to being sentenced to death row. It takes an in-depth look at their personal stories, shedding light on the circumstances and events that led to their conviction.

Processing into Death Row

Admitting prisoners onto death row involves a complex set of procedures and protocols that must be followed meticulously. This subchapter delves into the details of this process, providing an in-depth understanding of what happens when a prisoner is designated for death row.

Upon being sentenced to death, the prisoner is transferred to a maximum-security facility where death row is located. The first step in the processing is an initial assessment, which includes a thorough medical examination and evaluation of the inmate's mental state. This assessment helps determine the appropriate custody level and any specific needs the prisoner may have.

Next, the prisoner is assigned a cell on death row, where they will spend the remainder of their days. These cells are typically small, stark and isolated from the rest of the prison population. The motif is often one of strict confinement, emphasising the severity of their sentence.

Once settled in their cell, the prisoner becomes part of a highly structured routine. They are subject to strict security measures, including regular strip searches and constant surveillance. They are only allowed limited visitation and contact with the outside world. The prisoners spend most of their days confined to their cells, with limited opportunities for exercise and recreation.

A crucial aspect of processing into death row is the development of an individualised case plan for each prisoner. This involves determining their educational, vocational and therapeutic needs. The goal is to provide opportunities for personal growth and rehabilitation, despite the grim circumstances. Programs and counselling services are offered to address emotional and psychological concerns, aiming to support prisoners in finding meaning and purpose during their time on death row.

Processing into death row is an emotionally and psychologically challenging experience, not just for the prisoners, but also for the staff involved in their care. The transition from the general prison population to death row brings with it a sense of finality and impending doom. The weight of their impending execution can have a profound impact on prisoners' mental health, leading to depression, anxiety and even self-harm.

It is important to recognise the humanity and dignity of those on death row amidst the harsh realities they face. Themes of love, compassion and redemption can still emerge, making it imperative for prison staff to strive for empathy and understanding. While the circumstances are stark and difficult, providing support and opportunities for personal growth can contribute to the overall well-being of individuals awaiting their fate on death row.

The Reality of Sentencing

Being sentenced to death is a grim reality that brings despair and uncertainty into the lives of those condemned. The weight of such a sentence is incomparable, as it is literally a matter of life or death.

When someone is handed a death sentence, their entire existence is upended. They are stripped of their freedom and subjected to a life confined within the walls of a prison cell. The harsh reality of death row becomes their new reality, where every passing day serves as a painful reminder of their impending fate.

Living on death row is a daunting experience, marked by isolation, fear and a constant battle with one's own emotions. The condemned individuals are thrust into a world where they face the harshness of prison life alongside the constant reminder of their own mortality. The threat of execution looms over them like a dark cloud, casting a shadow of despair and anxiety over their day-to-day existence.

However, amidst the bleakness of life on death row, there are stories of love, compassion and redemption that emerge. Despite their circumstances, these individuals find solace in connecting with others and discovering glimmers of hope and humanity within the confines of their confinement.

The journey of a death row inmate is not just a tale of punishment; it is a battle for survival, perseverance and the search for meaning. The harshest realities of life on death row are juxtaposed with moments of profound reflection, self-discovery and personal growth. It is in these moments that the condemned individuals find the strength to confront their past, seek forgiveness and even experience redemption.

The story unfolds against a backdrop of profound injustices within the criminal justice system. It sheds light on the flaws and biases that lead to wrongful convictions and the devastating consequences they have on innocent lives. It also highlights the critical importance of eradicating these injustices and fostering a system that prioritises fairness, compassion and rehabilitation.

As we delve into the reality of sentencing, it is crucial to approach these stories with empathy and understanding. The individuals on death row are not just faceless statistics; they are complex human beings with dreams, aspirations and the capacity for change. Their stories remind us of the power of compassion, forgiveness and the potential for redemption in even the darkest of circumstances.

Chapter 2
Surviving the Isolation

The Solitary Confinement Experience

Imagine being locked away in a tiny cell with no human contact for days, weeks, or even years. This is the harsh reality of solitary confinement. In this subchapter, we will dive into the depths of the solitary confinement experience, exploring the psychological effects it has on individuals and the toll it takes on their mental health.

Isolation and solitary confinement can have devastating effects on a person's psychological well-being. Humans are social creatures, and the absence of human contact can lead to feelings of extreme loneliness, depression and anxiety. Research has shown that extended periods of isolation can cause hallucinations, cognitive decline and even suicidal tendencies. The mind, deprived of stimulation and interaction, begins to deteriorate, and the toll it takes on one's mental health is profound.

Now, let's delve into the experiences of individuals who have endured solitary confinement. Their stories shed light on the unimaginable challenges they faced and the resilience they showcased in the face of extreme isolation.

Meet John, a man who spent five years in solitary confinement. He entered the system as a young man, filled with anger and resentment. However, as the days turned into months and the months turned into years, John underwent a profound transformation. Alone with his thoughts, he found solace in writing. Words became his companions, and through poetry and prose, he connected with something deeper within himself.

Another inmate, Sarah, described her time in solitary confinement as a constant battle with her own mind. The lack of human contact intensified her feelings of despair, causing her to question her existence and lose sight of her own identity. However, amidst the darkness, she discovered a remarkable strength. Through self-reflection and a newfound appreciation for the simplest joys, Sarah managed to find moments of happiness even in the depths of her isolation.

These stories are not meant to romanticise the suffering endured in solitary confinement, but rather to humanise the experiences of those who have lived through it. They serve as a reminder of the capacity for love, compassion and redemption, even in the most challenging of circumstances.

In the next chapter, we will explore strategies to cope with the extreme loneliness and lack of human contact in solitary confinement. These strategies offer hope and guidance for individuals who find themselves in isolation, as well as insights for those seeking to understand the human spirit in the face of adversity.

Mental Health Challenges

Death row is a place where individuals face unique mental health struggles that are unparalleled in any other setting. The combination of isolation, uncertainty and impending execution takes a heavy toll on the psychological well-being of prisoners. In this section, we will delve into the mental health challenges faced by those on death row and shed light on the importance of providing appropriate support.

Life on death row is characterised by extreme isolation and a perpetual state of uncertainty. Prisoners spend most of their days confined to small cells, with limited human interaction and no access to the outside world. This heightened sense of isolation can lead to severe mental health issues, such as depression, anxiety and even psychosis.

The constant looming threat of execution adds another layer of psychological distress. Death row inmates live with the knowledge that their lives could be taken away at any moment. This uncertainty and anticipation can cause extreme stress, leading to a myriad of mental health disorders.

Moreover, the harsh realities of life on death row exacerbate existing mental health conditions. Many individuals who end up on death row have faced traumatic experiences, including abuse, neglect and violence. These experiences can contribute to the development of disorders such as post-traumatic stress disorder (PTSD), which further compounds the mental health challenges faced by prisoners.

Providing appropriate mental health support for those on death row is not just a matter of compassion; it is a fundamental human right. Despite the crimes they may have committed, prisoners are still entitled to receive adequate mental health care. This support not only helps in alleviating their suffering but can also contribute to a more just and humane criminal justice system.

Mental health professionals play a crucial role in addressing the unique mental health struggles faced by prisoners on death row. They are not only responsible for identifying and diagnosing mental health disorders but also for providing therapeutic interventions and support. Rehabilitation and treatment should be at the forefront of prison mental health programs, as they have the potential to bring about positive change and transform the lives of individuals.

It is imperative that we recognise the humanity of those on death row and acknowledge the profound impact that their mental health struggles have on their overall well-being. By providing appropriate mental health support, we can not only address their individual needs but also work towards creating a more compassionate and just society.

Finding Hope in Desolation

Amidst the bleakness of death row, there are stories of resilience and hope that shine like beacons in the darkness. These stories remind us of the indomitable spirit of the human soul, even in the face of impending doom. In this subchapter, we delve into the theme of finding hope in desolation on death row, and explore the sources of inspiration and motivation for the condemned.

The stories of those living on death row are often filled with unimaginable despair and loneliness. Yet, within the depths of such desolation, we find individuals who manage to discover hope. Their stories serve as a testament to the power of the human spirit and its ability to triumph over adversity.

One such story is that of John, a death row inmate who, despite being confined to a small cell for twenty-three hours a day, found solace in the art of writing. Through his words, he managed to escape the confines of his physical surroundings and delve deep into the recesses of his mind. His writing became a form of catharsis, a way for him to express his innermost thoughts and emotions.

John's story is a powerful reminder that even in the most dire circumstances, there is still room for creativity and self-expression. It showcases the resilience of the human spirit and the capacity for hope, even in the face of impending death.

Love, compassion and redemption are universal themes that transcend the boundaries of life on death row. Despite being surrounded by the harsh realities of their existence, inmates have the capacity to experience and cultivate these emotions.

An example of this is the story of Sarah, a death row inmate who found love and companionship in a fellow prisoner. Their relationship, though unconventional and restricted by the prison walls, served as a source of solace and support. It brought a glimmer of light into Sarah's otherwise dark and isolated world.

Sarah's story speaks to the enduring power of love and compassion, even in the most inhospitable of environments. It shows that despite the circumstances, humanity can still thrive and find ways to connect and provide comfort.

Redemption is another powerful theme that emerges amidst the harsh realities of life on death row. Many inmates use their time in confinement to reflect on their past actions and seek reconciliation and forgiveness.

One such story is that of Mark, a death row inmate who, through his spiritual journey, managed to find redemption and inner peace. He turned to religion and found solace in his faith, seeking forgiveness for his past mistakes. This newfound sense of purpose and spiritual growth transformed Mark's life, even within the confines of his cell.

Mark's story serves as a reminder that redemption is always possible, even in the darkest of circumstances. It highlights the transformative power of self-reflection and the pursuit of inner growth.

In conclusion, the subchapter *Finding Hope in Desolation* explores the stories of resilience, love, compassion and redemption amidst the harsh realities of life on death row. Through these narratives, we witness the indomitable spirit of the human soul, as it seeks hope and meaning even in the face of impending death. This subchapter serves as an exploration of the human capacity for resilience and the enduring power of hope, love and redemption.

Chapter 3
Bonds Behind Bars

Familial Relationships

The impact of death row on familial relationships is a subject of great significance and complexity. This subchapter aims to examine the various ways in which the condemned and their families are affected by this grim reality.

Familial relationships play a crucial role in the lives of individuals on death row. While the impending loss of a loved one can create immense pain and sorrow, it is paramount to explore the underlying dynamics within these relationships and how they evolve in the face of adversity.

Love, compassion and redemption are profound themes that emerge amidst the harsh realities of life on death row. Families of the condemned often grapple with conflicting emotions, struggling to reconcile their love for their incarcerated loved one with the crimes they were convicted of. It is a constant battle for forgiveness, understanding and finding a way to maintain a sense of connection.

Despite the staggering challenges, familial relationships have the potential to endure and even grow stronger in the face of adversity. The unique circumstances surrounding death row offer opportunities for families to display unwavering support, loyalty and compassion. By standing by their loved ones, families can become a vital source of comfort, hope and strength.

It is important to recognise that every familial relationship is unique, and the impact of death row will vary significantly. Some families may harbour anger and resentment, while others may focus on forgiveness and healing. Regardless of the path they choose, these families are bound together by the shared experience of navigating the tribulations of death row.

Through shared sorrow, families can become powerful advocates for change and justice. Their experiences can shed light on the flaws in the criminal justice system and the urgent need for reform. By speaking out against the injustices they witness firsthand, families can contribute to a larger movement that endeavours to create a more compassionate and equitable society.

Friendships in a
Hostile Environment

In the challenging environment of death row, where individuals face the impending reality of their execution, the development of friendships and alliances takes on a profound significance. Despite the grim circumstances, the human spirit has a remarkable capacity to seek connection and form bonds even in the most hostile of settings. This subchapter delves into the power of friendship within the confines of death row and the impact it has on those who face this harsh reality.

Within the walls of a prison, friendships become a lifeline—offering support, empathy and a sense of belonging. In a world of isolation and despair, these friendships serve as a light in the darkness, providing solace and helping inmates cope with the emotional and psychological toll of their circumstances.

Despite the inherent competition and tension that exists within the confines of death row, inmates find ways to establish meaningful connections with one another. They offer support and understanding, lending an empathetic ear in times of distress. These friendships offer a glimpse of humanity amidst an environment characterised by dehumanisation and despair.

Additionally, the bonds forged within the walls of death row provide a sense of belonging and camaraderie. Inmates form alliances, looking out for each other and working together to navigate the challenges of their shared circumstances. These relationships offer a rare source of support and validation, fostering a sense of unity and community amidst a hostile and isolating environment.

This subchapter delves into the complexities of friendships within death row, exploring the unique challenges and rewards of forming and maintaining social bonds in such extreme conditions. The story also explores the themes of love, compassion and redemption amidst the harsh realities of life on death row. Through the lens of these friendships and alliances, we gain a deeper understanding of the resilience and capacity for connection that exists within the human spirit, even in the most challenging of circumstances.

Romantic Connections on Death Row

In the confined and restricted setting of death row, where lives are marked by darkness and despair, the idea of love may seem like an unlikely occurrence. However, amidst the harsh realities, stories of romance and connection have emerged from these unlikely circumstances. These relationships offer a glimpse into the complexities and dynamics of human connections formed in the face of death.

Love knows no boundaries, and even in the most challenging environments, it finds a way to flourish. Within the walls of death row, inmates have managed to form deep and meaningful romantic connections with one another. These relationships, forged through shared experiences and shared emotions, provide a sense of solace and companionship in an otherwise isolating and desolate environment.

Within the confines of death row, moments of joy and happiness are scarce. Yet, love has the power to bring light to even the darkest corners of this grim reality. The bonds that form between individuals on death row are often built on a foundation of understanding and empathy, as they navigate the complexities of their shared circumstances. These relationships offer a glimmer of hope and a respite from the constant despair that surrounds them.

While the challenges are abundant, love on death row also brings its own unique set of joys and rewards. The knowledge that someone cares deeply for you, despite the circumstances, can be a source of tremendous comfort and support. In a world that seems to have turned its back on those sentenced to death, these romantic connections offer a sense of belonging and validation.

Love, compassion and redemption are powerful themes that emerge from these stories of romantic connections on death row. They showcase the resilience of the human spirit and the capacity for love in even the harshest of environments. These stories remind us of the importance of empathy and understanding in the face of adversity.

In conclusion, the subchapter *Romantic Connections on Death Row* delves into the complexities and dynamics of romantic relationships formed in the confines of death row. It explores the challenges and joys experienced by individuals who find love in such a confined and restricted setting. These stories shine a light on the power of love, compassion and redemption amidst the harsh realities of life on death row.

Chapter 4
The Legal Battle

Appeals and Advocacy

When it comes to death row inmates, the process of filing appeals and engaging in legal advocacy is a complex and challenging endeavour. It requires dedicated individuals who are committed to seeking justice for those who may have been wrongfully convicted. In this subchapter, we will delve into the intricacies of appeals and advocacy, outlining the steps involved in fighting for the rights of death row inmates.

One of the first steps in the process is understanding the grounds for appeal. Appeals are typically based on legal errors that may have occurred during the trial or sentencing phase. These errors can range from improper jury instructions to ineffective assistance of counsel. Death row inmates and their legal representatives must carefully review the case to identify any potential grounds for appeal.

Once the grounds for appeal have been identified, the next step is to file a notice of appeal. This document formally notifies the court and the prosecution that the defence intends to challenge the conviction or sentence. Filing a notice of appeal is time-sensitive and must be done within a specified period after the judgement is entered.

After the notice of appeal has been filed, the appellate process begins. This involves preparing briefs that outline the legal arguments supporting the appeal. These briefs must be well-researched, persuasive and backed by sound legal reasoning. It is crucial for lawyers to present a compelling case that highlights any errors or injustices that may have occurred during the trial.

Once the briefs have been submitted, the case moves to the appellate court. Here, the court will review the arguments presented by the defence as well as the prosecution's response. The appellate court may also hear oral arguments from both sides before making a decision. It is important for defence attorneys to effectively articulate their arguments and advocate for their clients' rights.

In addition to the formal appeals process, advocacy plays a significant role in seeking justice for death row inmates. Lawyers and organisations dedicated to this cause work tirelessly to bring attention to potential miscarriages of justice. They may conduct investigations, gather new evidence and collaborate with other stakeholders to shed light on cases that warrant further scrutiny.

Furthermore, legal advocacy for death row inmates goes beyond the confines of the courtroom. It involves raising awareness about the flaws inherent in the criminal justice system and advocating for broader societal changes. Lawyers and organisations may engage in public education campaigns, foster partnerships with other advocacy groups and seek legislative reforms that address the systemic issues that contribute to wrongful convictions.

Overall, the process of filing appeals and engaging in legal advocacy for death row inmates is an arduous one. It requires expertise, dedication and a deep commitment to justice. However, it is through these efforts that love, compassion and redemption can be found amidst the harsh realities of life on death row.

Facing the Legal System

The journey through the legal system is fraught with challenges and obstacles, often leaving individuals feeling overwhelmed and powerless. In this subchapter, we will explore the various difficulties faced by individuals as they navigate the complexities of the legal system.

When it comes to facing the legal system, individuals can encounter a multitude of challenges. From understanding complex legal procedures to finding adequate representation, the path can be arduous and confusing.

One of the main challenges faced is the lack of access to legal assistance. Many individuals, especially those from disadvantaged backgrounds, struggle to find affordable legal representation. This creates a significant disparity in their ability to present a strong defence.

Another obstacle is the lengthy and convoluted legal process. Court cases can drag on for months or even years, causing immense stress and uncertainty for those involved. The delays in the system can also lead to a loss of evidence or faded memories, hindering the pursuit of justice.

Moreover, the complexity of legal language and jargon can further complicate the situation. Individuals without a legal background may struggle to understand the intricacies of their case, making it difficult to effectively participate in their own defence.

When it comes to death row inmates, the legal system often reveals stark disparities and unfairness. These individuals are faced with a unique set of challenges that go beyond the difficulties encountered by others.

Firstly, death row inmates frequently come from disadvantaged backgrounds, lacking the financial resources to mount a strong defence. This leads to a disparity in the quality of legal representation they receive compared to individuals who can afford top-tier lawyers.

Racial and socio-economic biases also play a significant role in the unfairness experienced by death row inmates. Studies have shown that individuals from marginalised communities are more likely to be sentenced to death compared to their counterparts from privileged backgrounds. This highlights a grave injustice within the legal system.

Additionally, the limited avenues for appeal can further perpetuate the disparities faced by death row inmates. The high threshold of proof required for successful appeals makes it incredibly challenging to overturn a death sentence. This places a heavy burden on inmates seeking justice.

This subchapter sheds light on the difficulties encountered within the legal system and the disparities often faced by death row inmates. It is crucial to recognise these injustices and work towards a more equitable and compassionate legal system.

Throughout the story, we will delve deeper into these themes, exploring the power of love, compassion and redemption amidst the harsh realities of life on death row.

The Frustration of Legal Delays

Life on death row is a grim and harsh reality, where inmates face not only the prospect of their impending demise but also the emotional toll of prolonged legal delays and uncertainty. The waiting game that death row inmates endure can cause profound psychological distress. The constant anticipation of execution, coupled with the legal system's slow progress, can weigh heavily on their minds and lead to anxiety, depression and despair.

Living with the constant fear of death and the uncertainty surrounding one's fate can have devastating effects on mental health. It is essential to recognise and address the emotional impact of this prolonged legal process on death row inmates. Providing emotional support, counselling and therapy can help alleviate some of the psychological burdens they carry. Additionally, creating opportunities for meaningful human connection, through visits with loved ones or engaging in activities that promote self-expression and personal growth, can offer moments of solace and hope amidst the darkness.

The justice system is built on the principles of fairness, equality and timely resolution of legal matters. However, the reality often falls short of these ideals, especially when it comes to death penalty cases. The broken and slow-moving nature of the justice system has profound implications for individuals awaiting their fate on death row.

The frustration of legal delays can be overwhelming for both the accused and their loved ones. In many instances, the wheels of justice turn at a snail's pace, leading to prolonged periods of uncertainty and extended stays on death row. This not only creates psychological distress but also raises serious questions about the fairness and effectiveness of the justice system.

The themes of love, compassion and redemption become all the more significant amidst the harsh realities of life on death row. It is crucial to explore and understand these themes within the context of a broken justice system, where human lives are at stake. By shedding light on the implications and consequences of a slow and flawed legal process, we can strive for reforms that uphold the principles of justice and mercy.

Chapter 5
Acts of Kindness

Random Acts of Compassion

In the bleak and unforgiving world of death row, where despair and hopelessness often prevail, there are occasional glimmers of humanity that shine through the darkness. These glimmers manifest themselves in the form of random acts of compassion, small acts of kindness that provide momentary solace and human connection to those awaiting their ultimate fate.

Random acts of compassion can take many forms. They can be as simple as a smile from a prison guard, a comforting gesture from a fellow inmate, or an anonymous letter of support. These acts of kindness serve as reminders that even in the most dire of circumstances, there is still goodness and compassion to be found.

The stories of these random acts of kindness are both heartwarming and heart-wrenching. They depict the inherent humanity in both the giver and the receiver and showcase the power of empathy in the face of adversity. These stories remind us that even in the darkest places, love, compassion and redemption can thrive.

Love, the most powerful force in the world, can be found even in death row. It can be seen in the form of a family member who refuses to abandon their loved one, despite the heinous crimes they have committed. It can be seen in the unwavering support of a pen pal who offers words of encouragement and solace. It can be seen in the compassion of a prison chaplain who provides spiritual guidance and companionship to those who have been condemned.

Compassion, too, has its place in the world of death row. It can be seen in the small gestures of humanity that brighten an otherwise bleak existence. It can be seen in the shared meals and conversations between inmates, where the walls of isolation and despair are momentarily broken down. It can be seen in the mercy of a guard who treats the condemned with dignity and respect, recognising their intrinsic worth as human beings.

Redemption, perhaps the most profound theme that emerges from these stories, offers a glimmer of hope in a seemingly hopeless world. It is a reminder that no matter how far one may fall, there is always the potential for growth and change. Through acts of compassion and love, individuals on death row can find redemption in their own hearts and minds, and perhaps even in the eyes of society.

These stories of random acts of compassion are both a testament to the resilience of the human spirit and a call to action for all of us. They challenge us to look beyond the crimes committed and see the potential for transformation and growth in every individual. They urge us to extend a hand of kindness, even to those who have been cast aside by society. In doing so, we not only offer a lifeline to those on death row, but also reaffirm our own humanity and capacity for forgiveness.

Redemption Through Service

Acts of service and outreach have the incredible power to create opportunities for redemption. When individuals engage in selfless acts, they not only benefit others but also find a path towards personal growth and transformation. In this subchapter, we will explore the concept of redemption through service and how it offers a chance for individuals to find salvation and purpose.

Through the act of giving and helping others, individuals can experience a profound transformation within themselves. It is in those selfless moments that they discover the true essence of love, compassion and redemption. This subchapter delves into the beautiful narrative of redemption amidst the harsh realities of life on death row, highlighting the potential for change and growth that exists within every individual.

Impacts of Small Generosities

Life on death row is filled with despair, isolation and a constant reminder of impending death. In such a bleak setting, the value of small acts of generosity and compassion becomes even more profound. When individuals on death row receive even the smallest gestures of kindness, it can offer a glimmer of hope and humanity in their otherwise desolate lives. These acts, although seemingly insignificant, have the power to make a lasting impact on both the condemned and those who extend their generosity.

The impacts of small generosities extend far beyond the immediate recipients. Not only do the condemned individuals experience a renewed sense of dignity and worth, but the givers also experience a transformation within themselves. When individuals reach out and show compassion to those on death row, it serves as a reminder of the fundamental values of love, compassion and redemption. In that act of giving, they become a catalyst for change and hope amidst the harsh realities of life on death row.

Chapter 6
Facing Execution

Preparation for the End

The final days leading up to an execution on death row are filled with a range of emotions, both for the inmates awaiting their fate and for the prison staff involved in the process. As the countdown to the execution date begins, the inmates undertake various preparations to face the end.

Physically, the inmates focus on maintaining their health and well-being. They engage in regular exercise, often using the prison's limited facilities to stay fit. This physical activity not only helps them manage stress but also ensures their bodies are at their best during their final moments.

Emotionally, death row inmates often undergo counselling and therapy sessions to help them come to terms with their impending death. These sessions provide them with an opportunity to express their feelings, fears and regrets, allowing them to find closure and prepare emotionally for what lies ahead.

Furthermore, many inmates turn to their spiritual beliefs as a source of solace and strength. They may spend time praying, meditating, or engaging in religious rituals. This spiritual preparation helps them find inner peace and seek redemption for their past actions.

The final days leading up to an execution are marked by a series of rituals and practices that have developed over time within the prison system. These rituals serve to provide a sense of structure and comfort amidst the harsh reality of impending death.

One such practice is the granting of special privileges to the condemned inmate. They may be allowed to spend additional time with their loved ones, either through extended visitation hours or in-person meetings. This time together allows the inmate and their family to say their final goodbyes and find closure.

Another ritual involves the offering of a last meal to the inmate. This final culinary request is seen as a gesture of humanity, allowing the inmate to indulge in a meal of their choice before their execution. It serves as a symbolic act of compassion in the face of an otherwise grim reality.

Additionally, the prison staff may engage in a series of security procedures and final preparations. These include conducting last-minute checks on the execution equipment, ensuring all legal documentation is in order and coordinating with relevant personnel to ensure the smooth execution of the process.

Preparation for the End

The preparations made by death row inmates in the days leading up to their execution are not only physical, emotional and spiritual, but they also reflect their desire for closure, acceptance and, in some cases, redemption.

In the face of death, many inmates find solace in their connections with loved ones. They cherish every moment spent with family and friends, expressing their deepest love and gratitude. These final interactions serve as a profound reminder of the power of human connection and the significance of relationships.

Furthermore, the emotional and spiritual preparations undergone by death row inmates are a testament to the complexity of the human experience. They confront their past actions, seek forgiveness and strive for personal growth and transformation. For some, these preparations offer a pathway to redemption, an opportunity to make peace with themselves and their circumstances.

This subchapter aims to shed light on the intricate tapestry of emotions and rituals that accompany the final days on death row. Through exploring themes of love, compassion and redemption amidst the harsh realities of life on death row, we hope to foster deeper understanding and empathy for the individuals impacted by this challenging and highly complex legal system.

Last Words and Final Moments

When facing their final moments, those condemned to death often find solace in expressing their last words and thoughts. These poignant and profound statements offer a glimpse into the complex emotions that accompany their impending execution. As we delve into their final moments, we invite you to explore the depths of the human spirit and contemplate the weight of life and death.

The last words and thoughts of condemned individuals hold immense significance as they offer insights into the human condition and the harsh realities of life on death row. By examining these final moments, we can gain a deeper understanding of the depths of love, compassion and redemption that can emerge, even in the face of unimaginable circumstances.

Witnessing Executions

When it comes to the experience of witnessing an execution, it is a unique and profound event that can have a lasting impact on those involved. This subchapter aims to delve into the different perspectives and experiences of individuals who have witnessed executions, shedding light on the emotional and psychological aftermath that follows.

Witnessing an execution can be a highly intense and deeply personal experience. It brings individuals face to face with the grim reality of death and the complex ethical questions surrounding capital punishment. Those who find themselves in this position often have varying perspectives and reactions that are shaped by their own beliefs, values and prior experiences.

Some witnesses may support the death penalty and view the execution as a necessary act of justice. They may believe that witnessing the consequences of heinous crimes helps society to understand the gravity of such acts and serves as a deterrent to potential offenders. On the other hand, there are witnesses who are opposed to capital punishment, and for them, being present at an execution reaffirms their convictions against state-sanctioned violence.

Regardless of their stance on the death penalty, witnesses commonly describe feeling a mix of emotions before, during and after the execution. These emotions can range from anxiety and apprehension to sadness, relief, or even a sense of closure. Witnessing an execution can be a haunting and challenging experience that often stays with individuals for the rest of their lives.

Listening to the recounts of witnesses allows us to gain insight into the complexities surrounding capital punishment. It provokes thought and encourages a deeper examination of our own values and beliefs regarding justice and the sanctity of life.

Witnessing an execution can have profound psychological and emotional consequences for those involved. The impact of such an experience can vary greatly from person to person, as individual coping mechanisms and support systems play a significant role in determining how one processes and deals with the aftermath.

Some witnesses may experience symptoms of PTSD (Post-Traumatic Stress Disorder) following their involvement in an execution. Flashbacks, nightmares and emotional distress are not uncommon in these cases. Witnessing the deliberate taking of a life can leave a lasting imprint on the psyche, leading to long-term psychological difficulties.

Furthermore, witnesses may also grapple with feelings of guilt or moral conflict. Being complicit in the act of taking another person's life, regardless of their guilt or innocence, can provoke intense moral and ethical dilemmas. This internal struggle can have a profound impact on one's overall well-being and sense of self.

It is crucial for witnesses to have access to proper mental health resources and support systems to help them navigate the emotional aftermath of their experience. Therapy, counselling and community support groups can provide a space for witnesses to process their emotions, address any trauma and find support from others who have been through similar experiences.

Chapter 7
Aftermath for Loved Ones

Grieving and Finding Closure

In this subchapter, we will explore the intricate process of grieving and finding closure for family and friends of the condemned after an execution. The journey of grieving can be challenging, but it is an essential part of healing and moving forward.

Grief is a deeply personal experience that affects each individual differently. For those who have lost a loved one to the death penalty, the grieving process can be especially complex. It often involves a mix of emotions, including sadness, anger, guilt and confusion.

One of the challenges faced by family and friends is the stigma surrounding the condemned. Society often portrays them as monsters, making it difficult for their loved ones to share their grief openly. This can lead to feelings of isolation and shame.

It is important for family and friends to find support during this difficult time. Seeking therapy or joining support groups can provide a safe space to express emotions and share experiences with others who have gone through similar situations.

Another aspect of grieving is the search for closure. Closure does not mean forgetting or moving on; rather, it is the process of finding peace and acceptance after a loss. Closure can be found through various means, such as memorialising the loved one, engaging in rituals or ceremonies, or honouring their memory through charitable acts.

Each person's journey towards closure is unique and may take time. It is crucial to recognise that closure may not come in the form of complete resolution but rather in learning to live with the pain and finding ways to remember and honour their loved one.

This subchapter also explores the themes of love, compassion and redemption amidst the harsh realities of life on death row. It sheds light on the human aspects of both the condemned and their family and friends, reminding us that everyone is deserving of empathy and understanding, regardless of the circumstances.

Impact on Family and Friends

The impact of having a loved one on death row is profound and lasting. It is a situation that brings with it a wide range of emotions and challenges for both the individual facing execution and their family and friends left behind.

When a loved one is on death row, the emotional toll on their family and friends can be overwhelming. The uncertainty of their fate and the knowledge that their loved one is living under the constant threat of execution can cause immense stress, grief and anxiety. It is a burden that is carried with them every day, affecting their relationships, mental health and overall well-being.

Family and friends of individuals on death row often face stigmatisation and isolation from society. The weight of judgement and condemnation can be heavy to bear, as they are forced to navigate through a justice system that is often seen as flawed and inhumane. The ongoing legal battles, public scrutiny and media attention add to the already complex mix of emotions they experience.

However, amidst the harsh realities of life on death row, there are also stories of love, compassion and redemption. Families and friends often rally together to provide support, advocate for their loved one's rights and fight for justice.

They demonstrate extraordinary strength and resilience in the face of adversity.

Furthermore, the process of having a loved one on death row can lead to personal growth and a deepening of relationships. It forces individuals to confront their own beliefs about justice, forgiveness and the value of human life. The experience can be a catalyst for introspection and transformation.

In conclusion, the impact of having a loved one on death row is immense. The emotional toll on their family and friends is significant, as they navigate through a complex mix of emotions, stigma and challenges. However, amidst the difficulties, there are also stories of love, compassion and redemption. The experience can lead to personal growth and a deeper understanding of the complexities of life.

Remembering the Lost

is a solemn and significant task. It is important for us to remember and commemorate their lives, as well as acknowledge the injustices that accompanied their deaths.

Remembering the Lost allows us to reflect on the lives that were cut short and the impact they had on others. It is a reminder of the human cost of capital punishment and the need for compassion and understanding in our society.

Each individual who has been executed has a unique story, filled with love, compassion and redemption. Despite the harsh realities of life on death row, these individuals often found love and formed deep connections with others. Their stories are a testament to the enduring power of human connection and the resilience of the human spirit.

Through Remembering the Lost, we can honour these individuals by sharing their stories and ensuring that their lives are not forgotten. It is a chance for us to come together as a community and acknowledge the flaws in our justice system while striving for a more compassionate and equitable society.

Whether you have a personal connection to someone who has been executed or simply want to learn more about their experiences, Remembering the Lost serves as a tribute to their lives. It invites us to reflect on the complexities of capital punishment and the importance of empathy and understanding.

We can all play a role in ensuring that these lives are remembered and that we continue to work towards a more just society. By sharing their stories and advocating for change, we can honour their memories and strive for a future where the death penalty is no longer a part of our justice system.

Join us in Remembering the Lost and let us stand together in remembrance and commemoration.

Chapter 8
The Toll on Corrections Officers

Coping with The Job

Working as a corrections officer on death row can be an incredibly challenging and emotionally draining job. The psychological and emotional challenges faced by these officers are unique and require specific strategies for maintaining mental well-being in such a high-stress environment.

One of the key aspects of coping with the job is understanding the harsh realities of life on death row while still finding ways to maintain love, compassion and redemption within the confines of the prison walls.

One strategy for coping with the job is to find ways to humanise the individuals on death row. It can be easy to view them solely as perpetrators of heinous crimes, but it's important to remember that they are still human beings deserving of empathy and compassion. Building connections and finding common ground can help to foster a sense of understanding and even provide opportunities for rehabilitation.

Another important aspect of coping with the job is establishing a strong support system. This can include seeking out therapy or counselling services specifically tailored for corrections officers. Having a safe space to discuss one's experiences and emotions with a professional can be incredibly beneficial for mental well-being. Additionally, connecting with colleagues who understand the unique challenges of working on death row can provide a valuable support network.

Self-care is also crucial when it comes to maintaining mental well-being in this high-stress environment. Engaging in activities outside of work that bring joy and relaxation can help to counterbalance the emotional toll of the job. This can include hobbies, exercise, spending time with loved ones, or practicing mindfulness techniques.

In order to cope with the job, it's important for corrections officers to prioritise their mental well-being. This means recognising the signs of burnout and taking proactive steps to address and prevent it. It may involve seeking out additional resources, such as stress management workshops or peer support groups, to better equip oneself with the tools needed to navigate the challenges of working on death row.

Moral Dilemmas and Ethical Struggles

Working as a corrections officer in the execution process can be an emotionally and morally challenging role. These officers are tasked with carrying out the final and irreversible punishment of death on convicted criminals. While some may see it as justice being served, others find themselves facing deep moral dilemmas and ethical struggles.

These officers often grapple with questions such as the morality of taking a life, the possibility of wrongful convictions and the impact it has on their own mental well-being. The execution process forces them to confront conflicting emotions and beliefs.

A journey through the inner conflicts and personal reflections of corrections officers in the execution process reveals a complex web of emotions. From witnessing the final moments of a condemned person's life to questioning their own role in the justice system, these officers lead lives filled with doubts, turmoil and, ultimately, self-discovery.

The inner conflicts arise from the clash between their duty to the justice system and their own moral compass. Many officers find themselves torn between upholding the law and their own deeply held beliefs on the value of human life. They grapple with the weight of responsibility and the consequences of their actions.

Despite the harsh realities of life on death row, there are stories of love, compassion and redemption that emerge amidst the darkness. Officers form bonds with the condemned individuals they interact with daily, seeing them as more than just criminals. These relationships humanise both the officers and the prisoners, allowing for moments of empathy and compassion that defy the expectations of the environment.

Reflections on Serving
on Death Row

Working as a corrections officer on death row is an incredibly challenging and emotional role. These brave individuals have dedicated their lives to maintaining order, security and justice in a place where the consequences are unimaginable.

Reflecting on their experiences, corrections officers share stories of the deep impact that serving on death row has on their lives. They recount the moments of hope and despair, the bonds formed with inmates and the difficult decisions they face on a daily basis.

These personal reflections give readers a unique perspective into the world of death row and the complexities surrounding it. Through their stories, we gain insight into the human side of the justice system and the toll it takes on those who work within it.

Serving on death row is not an ordinary job. The emotional and psychological toll it takes on corrections officers is immense. This section delves into the long-term effects this role has on their lives.

Corrections officers often struggle with post-traumatic stress disorder (PTSD) and other mental health issues as a result of their experiences. They may face difficulties in their personal relationships and daily lives, haunted by the memories of witnessing executions and interacting with inmates on death row.

This subchapter aims to shed light on the often overlooked aftermath of working on death row. By exploring the long-term impact, readers gain a deeper understanding of the sacrifices made by corrections officers and the resilience they possess.

Reflections on Serving on Death Row

The reflections shared by corrections officers who have served on death row provide a raw and honest look into the realities of this challenging role. These stories offer a glimpse into the daily struggles and triumphs faced by those tasked with overseeing the lives of individuals condemned to death.

Through their experiences, corrections officers highlight the importance of compassion, love and redemption amidst the harsh realities of life on death row. Their stories encapsulate the complexities of the human condition and the potential for growth and transformation even in the darkest of circumstances.

Readers are invited to explore these reflections, empathise with the trials faced by corrections officers and gain a deeper appreciation for the inner workings of the justice system.

Chapter 9
Lessons from the Condemned

Insights on Life and Humanity

Welcome to the subchapter where we delve into the profound insights and reflections on life and humanity shared by death row inmates. Despite their circumstances, these individuals have experienced and learned valuable life lessons that they are eager to pass on.

While confined to death row, these inmates have had ample time to reflect on their lives, their choices and the world around them. Through their unique perspective, they offer us a glimpse into the deeper aspects of life that often go unnoticed.

Living on death row is an experience that few can imagine. It is a world filled with isolation, despair and uncertainty. Yet, amidst these harsh realities, some inmates have managed to find wisdom, love, compassion and even redemption.

One surprising theme that emerges from the stories of death row inmates is the presence of love and compassion in the most unlikely places. Despite their circumstances, some inmates have experienced profound connections with others, forming meaningful relationships and finding solace in shared experiences.

Another striking aspect of these stories is the potential for redemption and personal growth. The facing of their impending death often forces inmates to confront their past actions and make amends. Many have found solace in seeking forgiveness, whether it be from their victims' families or from a higher power.

In conclusion, the insights shared by death row inmates offer us a unique opportunity to reflect on our own lives and the essential aspects of humanity that we often take for granted. We can learn from their reflections and apply their wisdom to our own lives, fostering a greater sense of compassion, love and understanding.

Perspectives on Crime and Punishment

In this subchapter, we delve into the various perspectives on crime and punishment. Through the unique lens of those condemned to death, we gain insights into their thoughts and opinions. Amidst these tragic circumstances, thought-provoking ideas and alternative viewpoints emerge. Let's take a closer look at the themes explored in this subchapter.

The perspectives on crime and punishment that we encounter are diverse and thought-provoking. Each individual on death row has a unique viewpoint shaped by their own experiences and circumstances. Some may believe in the need for rigorous punishment, emphasising the importance of justice and deterrence. Others may advocate for rehabilitation and restorative justice, focusing on reform and addressing the root causes of criminal behaviour.

What makes these perspectives particularly intriguing is that they come from those who are facing the ultimate punishment—death. As outsiders looking in, it's important for us to understand these viewpoints that emerge from the most extreme circumstances. By doing so, we can gain a deeper understanding of the complexities surrounding crime and punishment.

As we explore these perspectives, we also encounter themes of love, compassion and redemption amidst the harsh realities of life on death row. The human capacity for transformation and the power of forgiveness are showcased, bringing hope and empathy to the forefront. These themes serve as a reminder that even in the darkest of situations, there is potential for growth and change.

Teachable Moments from Death Row

Within the experiences of death row inmates lie valuable lessons and teachable moments that can resonate with people from all walks of life. In exploring these stories, we find an opportunity for personal reflection and growth, while also considering the potential for societal change.

One of the most powerful aspects of delving into the world of death row is uncovering the teachable moments that emerge from these lived experiences. As we navigate through the stories of individuals facing their impending execution, we are forced to confront our own mortality and contemplate the value of life. In witnessing the resilience and strength exhibited by these inmates, we gain a newfound perspective on our own lives, appreciating the preciousness of each moment.

The stories from death row also highlight the importance of compassion and understanding. Despite the circumstances they face, many inmates find the capacity to demonstrate love and kindness towards others. Their ability to show compassion towards fellow inmates, prison staff, or even victims' families challenges our preconceived notions and prompts us to question our own capacity for forgiveness and empathy.

Additionally, the theme of redemption shines through in these narratives. Even in the face of their own mortality, many individuals on death row seek redemption and personal growth. Their stories teach us the transformative power of self-reflection and the endless potential for change, regardless of our past choices and actions.

By exploring the harsh realities of life on death row, we are confronted with the injustices that exist within our society. It prompts us to question our criminal justice system and the morality of capital punishment. Through these discussions, we foster a deeper understanding of the flaws within our society and work towards creating a more just and compassionate world.

The teachable moments from death row are not limited to a specific audience. They resonate with everyone, inviting us to reflect on our own lives, challenge our beliefs and seek opportunities for growth and change. These stories have the power to inspire, evoke empathy and transform our perspectives, reminding us of the importance of love, compassion and redemption in our own lives.

Chapter 10
Advocating for Change

Reforming the Justice System

Nowadays, the topic of the death penalty raises important questions about the fairness and efficacy of our criminal justice system. The use of capital punishment has always been a contentious issue, with passionate arguments on both sides. However, recent developments have shed light on the need for reform within the system.

Studies have shown that there is a significant risk of wrongful convictions in death penalty cases. The consequences of a wrongful execution are irreversible, and it is a grave miscarriage of justice. This risk alone should be enough to warrant a re-evaluation of our current system.

Moreover, there are troubling patterns of racial and socio-economic bias in death penalty cases. Studies consistently show that defendants who are members of racial minorities or who come from disadvantaged backgrounds are disproportionately sentenced to death. This raises serious concerns about equal treatment under the law and the potential for systemic injustice.

To ensure a fair and just criminal justice system, it is imperative that we examine the flaws within the current system and explore alternatives that prioritise rehabilitation and fairness over retribution.

With the flaws and injustices within the current criminal justice system brought to light, there have been various proposals for reform. These proposals aim to address the issues of wrongful convictions, racial bias and the overall fairness of the system.

One proposed change is the introduction of mandatory DNA testing in all death penalty cases. DNA testing has proven to be a powerful tool in exonerating wrongfully convicted individuals. By implementing mandatory testing, we can significantly reduce the risk of executing innocent people and further ensure the accuracy of our justice system.

Another alternative to the current system is the abolition of the death penalty altogether. Many argue that capital punishment is not only morally wrong but also ineffective as a deterrent. Instead of wasting resources on a flawed and costly system, they propose diverting those resources towards rehabilitation programs, education and mental health support for both victims and offenders.

It is important to note that these proposed changes do not discount the need for accountability for serious crimes. Rather, they aim to create a more just and humane system that focuses on rehabilitation, reintegration and addressing the root causes of crime.

As we explore further into the exploration of reform within the criminal justice system, we uncover the themes of love, compassion and redemption amidst the harsh realities of life on death row. The stories of those who have faced the prospect of execution invite us to question our own values and beliefs about punishment and forgiveness.

Love and compassion remind us of our shared humanity and the potential for transformation. They challenge us to seek alternatives to the death penalty that foster healing and growth, both for individuals and for society as a whole.

Redemption, too, plays a significant role in the conversation about criminal justice reform. It prompts us to consider the capacity for change and the possibility of second chances. By embracing a system that recognises and nurtures the potential for redemption, we can build a more compassionate and inclusive society.

Overall, the need for reform within the criminal justice system, particularly in relation to death penalty cases, is a pressing issue that demands our attention. By exploring proposed changes and alternatives, we can strive towards a more just, equitable and compassionate society.

Campaigning for Abolition

Over the years, numerous organisations and individuals have dedicated their time and resources to raising awareness and advocating for the abolition of the death penalty. These campaigns aim to shed light on the flaws and injustices associated with capital punishment and to promote alternative forms of punishment that prioritise rehabilitation and reform. Through initiatives such as public demonstrations, educational programs and lobbying efforts, these activists have sparked important conversations around the world.

The call for the abolition of the death penalty is fuelled by a multitude of reasons and arguments. Many argue that capital punishment violates the fundamental human right to life and goes against the principles of justice and fairness. They assert that the judicial system is fallible and has led to the wrongful execution of innocent individuals in the past.

In addition, opponents of the death penalty emphasise the inherent cruelty and inhumanity of taking a person's life as a form of punishment. They argue that it perpetuates a cycle of violence, rather than addressing the root causes of crime or offering opportunities for redemption and rehabilitation.

Campaigning for Abolition

Campaigns for the abolition of the death penalty have been instrumental in raising public awareness and mobilising support. These campaigns often employ various strategies to highlight the flaws and injustices of capital punishment and engage with the public on a personal level.

One common approach is to share the stories and experiences of individuals who have been wrongly sentenced to death or have faced the harsh realities of life on death row. These personal narratives humanise those affected by the death penalty, allowing the public to connect with their experiences and challenge their preconceived notions.

Furthermore, campaigners often organise events such as rallies, marches and panel discussions to gather like-minded individuals and amplify their collective voices. By coming together, they are able to create a sense of unity and show the authorities that there is a significant opposition to capital punishment.

Another effective strategy is to utilise social media platforms to spread awareness and educate the public about the flaws of the death penalty. Through compelling content, campaigners can reach a wide audience and encourage individuals to question their support for capital punishment.

Overall, the campaigning efforts for the abolition of the death penalty have been crucial in challenging the status quo and advocating for a more compassionate and just society. By highlighting the flaws of capital punishment and promoting alternative forms of punishment, these campaigns have made significant strides towards achieving their goal.

Supporting Reintegration Programs

In this subchapter, we will delve into the importance of supporting reintegration programs for former death row inmates. The journey of a death row inmate does not end upon their release from prison. Instead, it marks the beginning of a new chapter in their lives, one that requires immense support and resources to navigate.

Re-entering society after spending years locked away on death row is a daunting task. These individuals have not only faced the harsh realities of life in prison but have also had to confront the looming presence of death. It is crucial that we recognise the significance of providing support to help them reintegrate into society and seek redemption.

Reintegration programs play a vital role in assisting former death row inmates in finding their foothold in the outside world. These programs offer a range of support and resources tailored to the unique needs of individuals who have gone through such a traumatic experience.

One key aspect of reintegration programs is providing mental health and emotional support. Death row inmates have likely experienced severe trauma, isolation and psychological distress during their time in prison. Through counselling and therapy, they can begin to heal their emotional wounds, develop coping strategies and forge healthier relationships with others.

Another essential component of reintegration programs is offering educational and vocational training. Many former death row inmates may have been incarcerated for a significant portion of their lives, missing out on crucial educational and vocational opportunities. By providing them with access to education and skills training, we can empower them to acquire the knowledge and abilities needed to secure employment and become self-sufficient members of society.

Furthermore, reintegration programs must address the challenge of housing and homelessness. Upon release, former death row inmates often face difficulties finding stable housing due to various barriers, including financial limitations and social stigma. By collaborating with housing organisations and implementing housing initiatives specifically designed for this vulnerable population, we can help eliminate this barrier and provide them with a stable foundation to rebuild their lives.

Lastly, community support and acceptance are integral to successful reintegration. Often, former death row inmates are met with societal prejudice and discrimination, making it challenging for them to reintegrate successfully. By fostering a compassionate and inclusive society, we can create an environment that encourages acceptance and provides opportunities for former death row inmates to rebuild their lives.

In conclusion, supporting reintegration programs for former death row inmates is of utmost importance. By providing the necessary support and resources, we can help them heal, gain education and skills, secure stable housing and find acceptance within society. It is through these acts of love, compassion and redemption that we can help these individuals leave their past behind and embrace a brighter future.

Chapter 11
Finding Forgiveness

Personal Journeys of Forgiveness

We will explore the incredible power of forgiveness through the personal stories of individuals who have found the strength to forgive those responsible for the deaths of their loved ones. These stories serve as powerful examples of the human capacity for compassion, understanding and healing.

One such story is that of Sarah Johnson, a remarkable woman who experienced unimaginable pain and loss when her husband was tragically killed in a hit-and-run accident. Faced with overwhelming grief and anger, Sarah embarked on a journey towards forgiveness that would forever change her life.

Through years of therapy, self-reflection and support from her community, Sarah found the courage to let go of her resentment and embrace forgiveness. She realised that holding onto anger only continued to hurt her and that forgiving the person responsible allowed her to find peace and move forward.

This story showcases the incredible strength of the human spirit in the face of immense pain. It highlights the transformative power of forgiveness and how it can lead to redemption, not only for the person forgiving but also for the person who caused the harm. Sarah's story is a testament to the fact that forgiveness is a choice, and by making that choice, we can find healing and love amidst even the harshest realities of life.

Another remarkable story is that of Mark Jenkins, who lost his sister to a senseless act of violence. Devastated and consumed by feelings of anger and revenge, Mark's life seemed to spiral out of control. However, a chance encounter with a former gang member in a rehabilitation program would forever change his perspective.

As Mark shared his story and pain with this unlikely mentor, he began to see the humanity in the person who had taken his sister's life. He realised that violence begets more violence, and that forgiveness was the key to breaking the cycle. Through their deep conversations and shared experiences, Mark found empathy and compassion for the person who had caused him so much pain.

Mark's story teaches us that even in the darkest times, compassion can be found in unexpected places. It shows us that forgiveness has the power to heal not only ourselves but also those who have caused us harm. Mark's journey reminds us that forgiveness is an act of strength and courage, and that by embracing it, we can find redemption and create a more compassionate world.

Challenges in Forgiving

Forgiveness is a deeply personal and complex journey that individuals embark on in order to heal their emotional wounds and find inner peace. However, this path is often strewn with a myriad of challenges that can make the process arduous and overwhelming. Let's delve into some of the key challenges in forgiving:

Facing the fear of vulnerability: Forgiving someone means opening ourselves up to the possibility of being hurt again. This vulnerability can be terrifying, as it requires us to let go of our defences and trust that the other person will not hurt us again. It takes immense courage to confront this fear and embrace forgiveness.

Dealing with the scars of betrayal: Betrayal can leave deep emotional scars that can be difficult to heal. The process of forgiving someone who has betrayed our trust requires us to confront these scars head-on, acknowledge the pain they have caused and work towards healing and letting go.

Breaking free from the cycle of blame: It is often easier to blame others for our pain and suffering rather than take responsibility for our own emotions. However, in the journey of forgiveness, we must let go of the need to blame and instead focus on healing ourselves. Breaking free from the cycle of blame is a crucial step towards forgiveness.

Forgiveness is not a linear process but rather a complex one that is riddled with emotional barriers and internal struggles. Here are some of the common challenges faced by individuals seeking to forgive:

Overcoming feelings of betrayal: The act of forgiveness often involves reconciling with someone who has betrayed our trust. This can be an incredibly difficult and emotionally challenging task, as it requires us to navigate the complicated emotions that come with betrayal.

Battling with resentment and bitterness: Holding onto resentment and bitterness only serves to poison our own hearts. However, letting go of these negative emotions can be a daunting task. It requires us to confront and process deep-seated anger and bitterness, which can be painful and overwhelming.

Struggling with self-forgiveness: Before we can extend forgiveness to others, we must first learn to forgive ourselves. This can be a challenging process, as we often hold ourselves to high standards and struggle with feelings of guilt and self-blame. Learning to forgive ourselves is an essential step towards finding peace.

Dealing with the fear of vulnerability: Forgiving someone means being vulnerable and opening ourselves up to the possibility of being hurt again. This fear of vulnerability can be a significant barrier to forgiveness, as it requires us to confront our deepest fears and trust that the other person has changed.

The Power of Redemption

The concept of redemption holds a remarkable power within the realm of forgiveness. It is the key that has unlocked the hearts of countless individuals, allowing them to find healing and reconciliation even in the most challenging circumstances. This subchapter delves into the transformative effects of redemption and explores inspiring stories of individuals who have found redemption in their lives.

One such story is that of John, a man who found himself on death row for a crime he did not commit. Despite being subjected to harsh realities and the weight of an unjust system, John never lost hope. He clung to the belief that redemption was possible, not just for himself but also for those around him.

John's journey showcases the immense power of love, compassion and redemption. Despite the darkness that surrounded him, he managed to cultivate a sense of love and forgiveness within his heart. Rather than allowing bitterness to consume him, he chose to show compassion to his fellow inmates, offering them support and understanding.

Through his acts of love and compassion, John became a beacon of hope, inspiring others to seek redemption and forgiveness in their own lives. His story serves as a testament to the transformative power of redemption, showing that even in the most dire circumstances, one can find healing and reconciliation.

The story of John and others like him teaches us that redemption is not confined to a specific set of circumstances or individuals. It is a universal concept that has the potential to touch the lives of all, offering hope and healing in the face of adversity.

Chapter 12
Impact on Communities

Community Responses to Executions

In times of executions on death row, communities are often faced with a range of emotional and conflicting responses. The news of an impending execution can create a polarised environment within a community, filled with both supporters and opponents of the death penalty. Individuals on both sides of the debate passionately express their opinions, leading to heated discussions and debates within the community.

For some community members, the execution represents a sense of justice served. They may argue that the weight of the crime committed by the death row inmate warrants such a punishment. These individuals may believe that the execution acts as a deterrent, preventing others from committing similar crimes and thus contributing to their community's safety.

On the other hand, there are community members who vehemently oppose the death penalty. They might argue that the execution violates the fundamental right to life and is an inhumane practice. These individuals often advocate for alternative forms of punishment, such as life imprisonment or rehabilitation programs, which they believe can address the root causes of crime and lead to a more compassionate society.

Amidst these varying responses, it is also crucial to

acknowledge the impact on the families and loved ones of both the victims and the death row inmates. Executions often magnify the pain and trauma experienced by these individuals, reigniting their grief and reopening old wounds. The ripple effects of an execution can be far-reaching, affecting not only the immediate families but also the broader community that supports and stands by them.

However, despite these differences in opinion and emotions, communities have the potential to come together and engage in meaningful dialogue. Open discussions can help foster understanding and empathy among community members, even if they may never fully agree on the issue. By actively listening to one another's perspectives and sharing personal experiences, individuals within the community can build bridges of compassion and unity amidst the tensions that arise due to executions.

The exploration of community responses to executions showcases the complexities of our society. It depicts the deeply ingrained values and beliefs that shape individuals' perceptions of justice and punishment. Love, compassion and redemption are often recurring themes that emerge amidst the harsh realities of life on death row. The stories of individuals who support and advocate for the perpetrators' rehabilitation highlight the potential for change and human growth, even in the darkest of circumstances.

By understanding and acknowledging the diverse responses within our communities, we can strive towards a more inclusive and compassionate society. It is through dialogue, empathy and a commitment to justice that we can navigate the complexities surrounding the execution of death row inmates and work towards a better future for all.

Healing and Unity Efforts

In communities affected by the death penalty, there has been a growing recognition of the need for healing and unity. Organisations and individuals have come together to create initiatives that foster understanding and promote unity among those impacted by this issue. These efforts aim to provide support, guidance and resources for affected communities as they navigate the complex emotions and challenges that arise from the death penalty.

One such initiative is the Healing Circles program, which brings together individuals who have experienced the loss of a loved one through the death penalty. These circles create a safe space for participants to share their stories, express their emotions and explore ways to heal and find closure. Through facilitated discussions and therapeutic activities, participants are able to connect with others who have had similar experiences and find strength in their shared humanity.

Another important initiative is the Community Reconciliation Project, which aims to promote understanding and reconciliation between victims' families and those on death row. Through face-to-face meetings and restorative justice practices, this project encourages dialogue and open communication between individuals who have been directly impacted by the death penalty. By fostering empathy and understanding, the project strives to break down barriers and create a path towards healing and reconciliation.

These initiatives also prioritise community education and awareness by organising workshops, seminars and community events. These events provide opportunities for community members to learn about the experiences of those affected by the death penalty and engage in discussions about ways to promote healing and unity. By raising awareness and fostering dialogue, these initiatives help to create an environment of compassion, support and understanding within affected communities.

While the death penalty is a complex and divisive issue, there are efforts being made to explore possibilities for reconciliation and understanding. By examining the stories and experiences of individuals on death row, we can gain insight into the human side of this issue, highlighting the themes of love, compassion and redemption amidst the harsh realities of life on death row.

One powerful example is the story of John, a man who has spent over two decades on death row. Through his story, we witness his transformation and his journey towards redemption. John's story humanises the face of those on death row, challenging the notion of us versus them and reminding us of our shared humanity.

John's story also sheds light on the power of love and compassion in the face of adversity. Despite the harsh conditions and constant uncertainty of life on death row, John has managed to find solace and strength through his relationships with others. Through acts of kindness, support and forgiveness, he has created a sense of community within the confines of his prison walls.

By exploring these stories and themes, we can open up a dialogue around the possibilities for reconciliation and understanding. It prompts us to question the effectiveness and morality of the death penalty and encourages us to seek alternative approaches that prioritise healing, compassion and second chances.

Shifting Perceptions on Crime and Punishment

The presence of death row within a community can have a profound impact on the perspectives that individuals hold regarding crime and punishment. In this subchapter, we will delve into the shifting perceptions that often arise when a community is faced with the reality of death row. The exploration of these topics will shed light on the broader societal implications and debates that surround this complex issue.

As individuals come face to face with the realities of death row, their perspectives on crime and punishment may undergo a significant shift. The close proximity to individuals awaiting their execution forces people to confront the harsh realities of the criminal justice system. In many cases, this exposure leads to a deeper understanding of the complexity and nuance surrounding crime and the need for punishment.

One of the key themes that emerge from these shifting perspectives is the inherent value of human life. Witnessing the presence of death row highlights the preciousness and fragility of life, prompting individuals to contemplate the ethics of capital punishment. This reflection often leads to questions about the fairness and efficacy of the death penalty as a means of justice.

Another aspect of shifting perceptions on crime and punishment is the exploration of love, compassion and redemption amidst the harsh realities of life on death row. The interactions and relationships formed between inmates and those who work within the criminal justice system can be transformative for both parties. The presence of death row opens up opportunities for empathy and understanding, challenging preconceived notions about the nature of crime and punishment.

Furthermore, the presence of death row within a community sparks a broader societal conversation about the purpose of punishment and the potential for rehabilitation. Many individuals begin to question whether the primary objective of the criminal justice system should be retribution or if there is a greater need for rehabilitation and reintegration into society. These discussions around the effectiveness of the death penalty pave the way for a more nuanced understanding of crime and punishment.

The presence of death row within a community can lead to significant shifts in perspectives on crime and punishment. This subchapter has explored the themes of love, compassion and redemption amidst the harsh realities of life on death row, highlighting the complexity and nuance of this pressing societal issue.

Chapter 13
The Human Side of Death Row

Expressing Emotions
in Confinement

Life on death row presents a myriad of challenges and opportunities when it comes to emotional expression. The harsh realities of confinement, the impending execution and the often isolated nature of death row can create a unique environment for inmates to navigate their emotions. In this subchapter, we will delve into the complexities of expressing emotions in such a confined space and explore the impact it has on the individuals involved.

Emotions are a fundamental part of the human experience, and despite the limitations of their environment, death row inmates are not exempt from the depths of their emotions. In this section, we will explore the multifaceted ways in which these emotions manifest and are experienced by inmates. From anger and frustration to love and compassion, we will delve into the vast spectrum of emotions that exist within the confined world of death row.

Expressing Emotions in Confinement

The expression of emotions is a deeply personal and individual experience, and this is no different for those living on death row. Despite the restricted physical boundaries, inmates find various creative outlets for self-expression. Through writing, art, music and even personal interactions, inmates manage to communicate their emotions to the outside world and to one another. We'll examine these unique modes of expression and delve into the impact they have on the emotional well-being of those living in confinement.

Within the confines of death row, love, compassion and redemption can seem like distant and unattainable concepts. However, even in this challenging environment, these themes find their way into the lives of inmates and have a profound impact. We'll dive into the stories of individuals who have experienced love and compassion, as well as those who have found redemption in the face of their impending fate. Through these narratives, we gain a deeper understanding of the resilience of the human spirit and the transformative power of these emotions even within the most unforgiving circumstances.

Creative Outlets and Artistic Expression

Life on death row is an environment filled with darkness, despair and isolation. Yet, amidst these harsh realities, there exists a glimmer of hope—artistic expression. Creative outlets have proven to be powerful tools in maintaining humanity and mental well-being for individuals facing the impending end of their lives.

In the face of limited resources and restricted freedoms, prisoners on death row often turn to artistic pursuits as a means of escape. Through drawing, painting, writing and other forms of creative expression, inmates find solace and freedom within the confines of their cells. Art becomes their sanctuary, a place where they can freely explore their thoughts and emotions, offering a glimpse into their inner worlds.

Artistic expression serves as a form of therapy for these individuals, allowing them to process trauma, confront their fears and express their deepest emotions. The act of creating art becomes a cathartic experience, providing a release from the weight of their circumstances. It allows them to channel their energy into something positive, finding beauty and meaning in their lives despite their dire circumstances.

In a place where communication is limited and emotions are suppressed, art becomes a powerful means of self-expression for those on death row. Through their artwork, these individuals can convey their thoughts, desires and dreams to the outside world. Art becomes a voice, a way to bridge the gap between their isolated existence and the world beyond the prison walls.

Not only does art provide a communication channel with the outside world, but it also fosters a sense of connection among those on death row. Inmates often form artistic communities, sharing their creative endeavours, exchanging feedback and supporting each other's artistic growth. These communities offer a sense of belonging and camaraderie, counteracting the feelings of loneliness and isolation that pervade life on death row.

Through their artwork, these individuals also have the opportunity to challenge societal perceptions and stereotypes associated with prisoners. They showcase their talents, proving that their humanity extends beyond their crimes. Art becomes a tool for redemption and a means of reclaiming their identities, as they strive to be seen and understood for who they truly are. Creative Outlets and Artistic Expression Within the confines of death row, creative outlets play a crucial role in preserving the humanity of those facing execution. Whether through painting, writing, or other forms of artistic expression, prisoners are able to find solace, channel their emotions and foster a sense of connection. Art becomes a lifeline, providing an escape from the darkness and offering hope amidst despair.

Love, compassion and redemption amidst the harsh realities of life on death row.

In the midst of a stark and unforgiving environment, love, compassion and redemption find a way to flourish within the hearts of those condemned to death. Despite the weight of their circumstances, these individuals have the capacity for deep and profound connections. Whether it be through their artistic endeavours, acts of kindness towards fellow inmates, or seeking redemption for their past actions, they embody the very essence of humanity.

This story explores the complex themes of love, compassion and redemption within the context of life on death row. It delves into the profound impact of artistic expression as a means of maintaining mental well-being and finding solace amidst the harshest of conditions. Through the lens of these individuals, we are reminded of the inherent capacity for goodness that resides within each of us, no matter the circumstances we may find ourselves in.

Maintaining Humanity
Amidst Struggles

Being on death row is an unimaginably difficult and dehumanising experience. Nevertheless, it is remarkable to witness the resilience and determination of those facing such adversity. Even in the face of death, these individuals find ways to maintain their sense of humanity and uphold their dignity.

One way in which they do this is by cultivating meaningful connections with others who share their struggles. Despite being confined within the walls of a prison, they manage to form bonds of love, compassion and support. These connections often become a source of strength and solace for those on death row, who find comfort in their shared experiences and the knowledge that someone understands and cares.

Moreover, they strive to engage in activities that give them a sense of purpose and self-worth. Although their circumstances may be limited, they find ways to contribute and make a positive impact. Through artistic expression, writing, or participating in educational programs, they tap into their creativity and intellectual capacity, reaffirming their worth as human beings.

Additionally, they actively seek out opportunities for self-reflection and personal growth. Despite their dire circumstances, they refuse to succumb to despair and instead focus on introspection and self-improvement. Through self-reflection, they gain a deeper understanding of themselves, confront their past actions and work towards personal redemption.

Preserving self-worth and maintaining a sense of personal identity is paramount for individuals on death row. Despite the dehumanising environment in which they find themselves, they fight to hold onto their humanity and individuality.

One way in which they do this is by actively asserting their innocence and challenging the system that has condemned them. By refusing to be defined solely by their crimes or their circumstances, they assert their right to be seen as more than a mere statistic. Their desire for justice and fair treatment reflects a fundamental belief in their own worth as individuals.

Furthermore, they focus on personal growth and education as a means of preserving their sense of self. Despite the limitations imposed upon them, many individuals on death row engage in educational activities and pursue knowledge. By honing their skills, expanding their intellectual horizons and discovering new interests, they find a way to assert their individuality and maintain a semblance of personal identity.

Moreover, they find solace and strength in maintaining relationships with loved ones outside of prison. By staying connected to their families, friends and communities, they reaffirm their ties to the outside world and preserve a sense of belonging and connection. These relationships offer them a lifeline to the human experiences and emotions that may feel distant or inaccessible within the prison walls.

Chapter 14
Voices of the Condemned

Personal Stories and Testimonies

The personal stories and testimonies shared by individuals on death row offer a unique perspective on life, love, compassion and redemption. Through their narratives, we gain a deeper understanding of the harsh realities they face and the complex emotions they experience.

These stories serve as powerful reminders of the humanity that exists within every individual, regardless of their circumstances. They compel us to question our own beliefs, values and biases, encouraging us to examine the criminal justice system and its impact on the lives of those awaiting execution.

Each personal story and testimony serves as a testament to the strength, resilience and vulnerability of the individuals on death row. Their accounts often reveal the injustices they have faced, the remorse they feel for their actions and their enduring hope for redemption.

By sharing these stories, we aim to foster empathy, understanding and dialogue. Through their own voices, these individuals provide profound insights into the complexities of life on death row, shedding light on the human experiences often overlooked or silenced by society.

Through the themes of love, compassion and redemption, we are confronted with the profound capacity for change and growth, even in the most challenging circumstances. These stories challenge our preconceived notions and invite us to consider the possibility of second chances, forgiveness and the power of empathy.

By offering a platform for these voices to be heard and understood, we hope to inspire meaningful conversations, advocate for justice and mercy and, ultimately, work towards a more compassionate and equitable criminal justice system.

Reflections on Wrongful Convictions

In this subchapter, we will reflect on wrongful convictions and the profound impact they have on individuals who have been wrongly sentenced to death. Through these reflections, we gain a better understanding of the themes of love, compassion and redemption that emerge in the midst of the harsh realities of life on death row.

Wrongful convictions are a grave injustice that have far-reaching consequences for those who experience them. Imagine being convicted and sentenced to death for a crime you didn't commit. The weight of such a sentence is unimaginable and can have a profound impact on a person's life. The process of examining wrongful convictions helps shed light on the flaws within our legal system and highlights the need for justice and reforms.

One of the key themes that emerges from these reflections is the resilience of the human spirit. Despite the despair and hopelessness that can accompany life on death row, individuals who have been wrongfully convicted often find the strength to continue fighting for their innocence. Their stories are a testament to the power of love and compassion, both within themselves and from the support networks that rally behind them.

Redemption is another powerful theme that emerges. As we reflect on wrongful convictions, we come to realise the immense importance of finding the truth and righting the wrongs of the legal system. When innocent individuals are released, they not only reclaim their freedom but also have the opportunity to rebuild their lives. Their resilience and ability to find redemption in the face of adversity is truly inspiring.

This subchapter on reflections of wrongful convictions allows us to delve deep into the emotions and experiences of those who have faced this grave injustice. Through their stories, we gain a renewed appreciation for the importance of justice, compassion and the need for reforms within the legal system.

Hope for the Future

Within the confines of death row, there lies a glimmer of hope for the future. In the face of unimaginable circumstances, the men and women awaiting their fate find strength in the belief that redemption and salvation are not beyond their reach. This subchapter delves into their stories, exploring the enduring power of hope amidst the harsh realities of life on death row.

The first theme that emerges from these narratives is love. Despite the isolation and despair that surrounds them, many individuals on death row maintain strong connections to their loved ones. From letters exchanged to visits behind thick glass barriers, these individuals find solace and support in the love they share with family and friends. In their darkest moments, the bonds of love sustain them and remind them of their inherent worth as human beings.

Compassion is another prevailing theme woven through the fabric of their stories. Surrounded by a system that is marked by judgement and punishment, the individuals on death row often encounter acts of kindness and understanding from unexpected sources. Whether it is a prison guard offering a small gesture of empathy or a fellow inmate extending a helping hand, these acts of compassion provide glimpses of light in an otherwise bleak existence.

Redemption, the ultimate goal for many on death row, serves as a beacon of hope. Despite their past actions and the consequences they face, these individuals strive for personal growth and transformation. Through education, therapy and self-reflection, they work towards becoming better versions of themselves, seeking redemption not only in the eyes of society but also within their own hearts. They refuse to be defined solely by their past, choosing instead to embrace the possibility of a different future.

In conclusion, the stories from death row reveal a profound resilience and spirit of hope that transcends the harsh realities of their circumstances. Love, compassion and redemption serve as guiding lights, reminding us of the power of the human spirit to find strength and purpose even in the face of seemingly insurmountable obstacles. These stories challenge us to examine our own preconceptions and beliefs, encouraging us to extend empathy and understanding to those who find themselves on the margins of society.

Chapter 15
Embracing Compassion

Acts of Mercy and Empathy

The subchapter *Acts of Mercy and Empathy* delves into the exploration of acts of mercy and empathy towards death row inmates. It sheds light on the transformative power of compassion in the pursuit of justice. This subchapter seeks to engage readers from all walks of life and emphasises the importance of showing empathy and mercy towards individuals facing such dire circumstances.

The story within this subchapter encompasses a range of emotions, from love and compassion to redemption, amidst the harsh realities of life on death row. It provides a glimpse into the human experience and challenges readers to consider the possibility of finding light in even the darkest of situations.

Embracing Restorative Justice

In this subchapter, we will explore the concept of restorative justice and explore its potential application within the context of death row. Restorative justice is a paradigm shift from traditional punitive measures, focusing on healing and reconciliation rather than punishment alone. It offers an alternative approach to addressing the complex issues surrounding crime, punishment and the restoration of individuals and communities affected by crime.

Restorative justice emphasises the importance of dialogue, empathy and understanding. It seeks to bring together victims, offenders and the community to foster dialogue and find ways to repair harm, rebuild relationships and promote healing. This approach can be particularly powerful in the context of death row, where the stakes are incredibly high and emotions run deep.

By embracing restorative justice in the realm of death row, we open up a space for meaningful conversations and opportunities for transformation. It challenges us to confront the harsh realities of life on death row and explore the themes of love, compassion and redemption. It asks us to consider how we, as a society, can approach punishment and reconciliation in a more humane and compassionate manner.

Love plays a crucial role in the restorative justice process. It urges us to look beyond the labels of victim and offender and recognise the inherent worth and dignity of every individual. Love reminds us that even those who have committed the most heinous crimes are capable of change and deserve a chance at redemption.

Compassion is another essential element of restorative justice. It compels us to put ourselves in the shoes of others, seeking to understand the pain and suffering experienced by victims and offenders alike. Compassion drives us to address the root causes of crime and work towards preventing future harm, rather than perpetuating a cycle of violence.

Redemption is a profound and transformative concept inherent in restorative justice. It acknowledges that individuals who have committed grave offences can rebuild their lives, make amends and contribute positively to society. It offers them a path towards redemption, allowing them to find meaning and purpose in their actions, even amidst the bleakness of life on death row.

As we venture further into the exploration of alternative approaches to punishment and reconciliation, let us embrace restorative justice with open hearts and minds. Together, we can challenge the prevailing systems and work towards fostering a more compassionate, healing-centred society, even within the confines of death row.

The Path to Healing and Reconciliation

The journey towards healing and reconciliation is not an easy one. It requires a deep understanding of the pain and suffering experienced by all parties involved in capital punishment cases—the condemned, the victims and society as a whole. But within this complex web of emotions and power dynamics, there lies an opportunity for transformation and growth.

One of the crucial steps in the path to healing and reconciliation is creating space for empathy and understanding. It is essential for all parties to recognise the humanity that exists within each individual. By acknowledging the shared experiences of joy, sorrow and love, bridges can be built to connect even the most divided hearts.

Another important aspect of this journey is accountability. While forgiveness is an integral part of the healing process, it is equally important not to forget the pain caused. Holding individuals accountable for their actions allows for justice to be served and ensures that the cycle of violence is not perpetuated.

Restorative justice practices can also play a significant role in fostering healing and reconciliation. These practices focus on repairing the harm caused by crime rather than simply punishing the offender. They provide an opportunity for dialogue, understanding and healing between the condemned, the victims and the broader community.

Furthermore, supporting the mental and emotional well-being of all parties involved is vital in this journey. Trauma-informed care and counselling services can help individuals process their pain, find inner peace and rebuild their lives. By investing in rehabilitation and support programs, we can create a path towards redemption for those who have committed grave mistakes.

Finally, education and awareness are key components of this healing process. We must strive to build a more compassionate future by challenging societal norms and biases that contribute to violence and division. By promoting empathy, love and understanding, we can work towards a society that values healing and reconciliation over revenge and punishment.

Through the themes of love, compassion and redemption, we can navigate the difficult terrain of life on death row and beyond. It is through these efforts that we can bring about healing and reconciliation, not only for the individuals directly affected by capital punishment but for society as a whole.